Best Jokes

& other humor from the

internet

VOLUME 1

Jon@than P. Sulliv@n

Castle
Pacific
Publishing

Washington, D.C.

ISBN 0-9653869-1-0
Library of Congress Catalog Card Number 97-067738

Printed on high recycle-content paper.

Inside

About This Book ...

Before the Internet, jokes were shared around the office water cooler, at the playground, in bars and at parties. A few enterprising individuals, my father included, would create more elaborate jokes on paper, mass produce and then mail or distribute them to friends and colleagues. If you haven't personally received one of these gems, I'm sure you've seen one tacked to the bulletin board in the company lunchroom.

In the modern age of digital communication, jokes, from one-liners to stories, are ever more frequently shared via e-mail. I would even say that the Internet is responsible for a renaissance in folk humor. Once again, jokes are part of the daily experience as more and more people put their ear to the ground of the Internet.

There are two purposes for this book. One is to demonstrate that the Internet is not all about indecency, extremism, and advertising, but rather about people communicating with one another. With this communications medium, as with all others before it, humor is a large part of that communication. The Internet newsgroup rec.humor.funny is the most widely read resource on the Internet today, according to Brad Templeton, the group's founder. Which brings us to the primary purpose of this book: to highlight the work of some unknown authors who in moments of brilliance, inspired by the day's events or one of life's little mysteries, created the best jokes (and other humor) from the Internet.

Most of the jokes and stories reprinted in this book are in their exact form from the Internet. A few have been reformatted for a better fit on the printed page. For instance, paragraph indents have been removed in some cases and a few more have had typos or spelling and grammar problems corrected where these problems draw attention away from the joke. Where the joke consists of a number of smaller jokes, I have also in a few cases needed to shorten the list (which probably grew and changed over time, anyway) by a few jokes to keep it within the scope of this book (that is, short, and truly the best of the Internet).

So enjoy! And drop me a line at jokes@castlepacific.com if you have any jokes you'd like to see added to the next edition (and let me know if you are the author, or if you know who the author is, so you/they can be properly thanked in the next acknowledgments section).

... And Those Who Made It Possible

would not have completed this book without the encouragement and shepherding of its publisher, Glenn Hampson. I am grateful to him for providing the initial spark and keeping it lit. Thanks to everyone who sent jokes from work and would get in trouble if their boss ever found out, especially Bill, Bruce, Drienna, Glenn, Jeff, Margaret, Mike, Paul, Peter, Ron, Ramzi, Sarah, Scott, Steve, and Steven. Cindy, Drienna, Kim, Paul, Ramzi, and Glenn were tremendously helpful in selecting the jokes that made it into the book and preventing it from becoming "Jonathan Sullivan's Favorite Jokes from the Internet." For that I am sure the reader is thankful.

A tip of the hat also to Paul Crystal for his editing input. I am indebted to Peter Abrahams and Richard Creighton at The Magazine Group for giving the book a chance with their enthusiasm and great design. Joan Grippo deserves our thanks for turning that design into the final product that you now hold in your hand.

Finally, I would like to thank my wife Cindy for the time and space in which this book was created.

Jon@than

To Jeff.

Thanks for the laughs over the years,
and don't let the milk come out of your nose
while reading this.

Recently In the News

Actual Headlines

1. Something Went Wrong in Jet Crash, Expert Says

2. Police Begin Campaign to Run Down Jaywalkers

3. Safety Experts Say School Bus Passengers Should Be Belted

4. Drunk Gets Nine Months in Violin Case

5. Survivor of Siamese Twins Joins Parents

6. Farmer Bill Dies in House

7. Iraqi Head Seeks Arms

8. Is There a Ring of Debris around Uranus?

9. Stud Tires Out

10. Prostitutes Appeal to Pope

11. Panda Mating Fails; Veterinarian Takes Over

12. Soviet Virgin Lands Short of Goal Again

13. British Left Waffles on Falkland Islands

14. Lung Cancer in Women Mushrooms

15. Eye Drops off Shelf

16. Teacher Strikes Idle Kids

17. Squad Helps Dog Bite Victim

18. Shot off Woman's Leg Helps Nicklaus to 66

19. Enraged Cow Injures Farmer with Ax

20. Plane Too Close to Ground, Crash Probe Told

21. Miners Refuse to Work after Death

22. Juvenile Court to Try Shooting Defendant

23. Two Soviet Ships Collide, One Dies

24. Two Sisters Reunited after Years in Checkout Counter

25. Killer Sentenced to Die for Second Time in 10 Years

26. Never Withhold Herpes Infection from Loved One

27. War Dims Hope for Peace

28. If Strike Isn't Settled Quickly, It May Last a While

29. Cold Wave Linked to Temperatures

30. Red Tape Holds Up New Bridge

31. Deer Kill 17,000

32. Typhoon Rips Through Cemetery; Hundreds Dead

33. Man Struck by Lightning Faces Battery Charge

34. New Study of Obesity Looks for Larger Test Group

35. Astronaut Takes Blame for Gas in Spacecraft

36. Kids Make Nutritious Snacks

37. Ban on Soliciting Dead in Trotwood

38. Lansing Residents Can Drop off Trees

39. Local High School Dropouts Cut in Half

40. New Vaccine May Contain Rabies

41. Prosecutor Releases Probe into Undersheriff

42. Old School Pillars Are Replaced by Alumni

Police in Wichita, Kansas, arrested a 22-year-old man at an airport hotel after he tried to pass two (counterfeit) $16 bills.

• • •

The Chico, California, City Council enacted a ban on nuclear weapons, setting a $500 fine for anyone detonating one within city limits.

• • •

A bus carrying five passengers was hit by a car in St. Louis. By the time police arrived on the scene, fourteen pedestrians had boarded the bus and had begun to complain of whiplash injuries and back pain.

• • •

A convict broke out of jail in Washington D.C. A few days later he accompanied his girlfriend to her trial for robbery. At lunch he went out for a sandwich. She needed to see him and thus had him paged by the bailiff. Police officers recognized his name and arrested him when he returned to the courthouse in a car he had stolen over the lunch hour.

• • •

When two service station attendants in Ionia, Michigan, refused to hand over cash to an intoxicated robber, the man threatened to call the police. They still refused, so the robber called the police and was arrested.

• • •

FBI agents conducted a raid on a psychiatric hospital in San Diego that was under investigation for medical insurance fraud. After hours of reviewing thousands of medical records, the dozens of agents had worked up quite an appetite. The agent in charge of the investigation called a nearby pizza parlor with delivery service to order a quick dinner for his colleagues.

The following telephone conversation took place and was recorded by the FBI because they were taping all conversations at the hospital.

Agent: Hello. I would like to order 19 large pizzas and 67 cans of soda.

Pizza Man: And where would you like them delivered?

Agent: We're over at the psychiatric hospital.

Pizza Man: The psychiatric hospital?

Agent: That's right. I'm an FBI agent.

Pizza Man: You're an FBI agent?

Agent: That's correct. Just about everybody here is.

Pizza Man: And you're at the psychiatric hospital?

Agent: That's correct. And make sure you don't go through the front doors. We have them locked. You will have to go around to the back to the service entrance to deliver the pizzas.

Pizza Man: And you say you're all FBI agents?

Agent: That's right. How soon can you have them here?

Pizza Man: And everyone at the psychiatric hospital is an FBI agent?

Agent: That's right. We've been here all day and we're starving.

Pizza Man: How are you going to pay for all of this?

Agent: I have my checkbook right here.

Pizza Man: And you're all FBI agents?

Agent: That's right. Everyone here is an FBI agent. Can you remember to bring the pizzas and sodas to the service entrance in the rear? We have the front doors locked.

Pizza Man: I don't think so.

Click!

Ebonics

PORTLAND, ME, Jan. 17.—In a move that has surprised educators nationwide, the Portland Board of Education announced today that, beginning February 1, all Portland schools will provide teacher and parent training in Yankee English, or so-called Yankonics, recognize Yankonics as distinct from standard English, and help Yankee children who use Yankonics to master standard English.

In its resolution, the Portland school board described Yankee English as a distinct language, rather than a dialect of standard English.

The district said it would not teach Yankonics, derived from the words Yankee and phonics, in place of standard English, and would not try to classify Yankonics-speaking students as bilingual in order to obtain federal funds.

Both the Clinton Administration and congressional Republicans moved quickly to attack the announcement, with the Administration emphasizing that it would refuse to grant special funding.

Reaction in the city was guarded, but supportive. Lobsterman John Nadeau, 43, of Fore St. said, "Every yeah it gets hahda and hahda for ouah kids to get the jawbs they need. I cahn't say if this will wohk oah nawt, but at least it's a staht."

The lunch crowd at Demillo's echoed Nadeau's position. Mary Lamoreaux, 54, of Falmouth Foreside concurred. "I've got two daughtahs, neithah of whom cahn undahstahnd hahlf the things they heah on TV. Something needs to be done."

Patrick Payson, 35, a developer at One City Center, admitted that he's found his linguistic heritage a difficult cross to bear at times. "I went down to New Yahk a few weeks ago foah some meetins. It took me close to two days to figuah out what people weah tahlking about. Rest assuahed, I was wicked confused when I gawt bahck."

Some, however, were not convinced. Arthur Wentworth, 87, a scrimshaw artist in the Old Port, said, "Deah Gawd. Yeahs ago no one cahed so much about this soht of thing, we just went on about ouah business. I don't see much use in this. If people from away cahn't understahnd what weah saying, then they just ought head back to Massasstwoshits, oah wheyevah they came frawm."

Asked if he'd lived in Portland all his life, Wentworth replied, "not yet."

The Trial (of the Century)

T he following ditty stems from **O.J.**'s statement to Judge Ito saying that he could not and would not have committed the crimes he was accused of committing (Ito's lines are in capital letters):

DID YOU DO THIS AWFUL CRIME?
DID YOU DO IT ANYTIME?

I did not do this awful crime
I could not, would not, anytime

DID YOU TAKE THIS PERSON'S LIFE?
DID YOU DO IT WITH A KNIFE?

I did not do it with a knife
I did not, could not, kill my wife
I did not do this awful crime
I could not, would not, anytime

DID YOU LEAVE A POOL OF BLOOD?
DID YOU DROP THIS BLOODY GLOVE?

I did not leave a pool of blood
I can not even wear that glove
I did not do it with a knife
I did not, could not, kill my wife

I did not do this awful crime
I could not, would not, anytime

I did not do it, so I say
It's not my blood or DNA
I did not kill my lovely wife
I did not slash her with her knife
I did not bonk her on the head
I did not know that she was dead

I stayed at home that fateful night
I took a cab, then took a flight
The bag I had was just for me
My bag! My bag! Leave it be!

When I came home I had a gash
My hand was gashed from broken glass
I cut my hand upon a glass
A broken glass did cause that gash

My friend, he took me for a ride
All through L.A., from side to side
From North to South, we took a ride
But from the cops, I could not hide

And now we've been here for a year
A year! A year! Just sitting here!
The DNA, the hem and haw
The circus-hype the viewers saw
A year! A year! Just sitting here!
And lawyers charge by the hour, I fear

If I'm found "Guilty," I'll appeal
Appeal! Appeal! I will appeal!
I'll wheedle and whine, I'll cut a deal!
If it's "Not Guilty," so glad I'll feel

Always
In the News

Religion & Philosophy

"WHY DID THE CHICKEN CROSS THE ROAD?"

TIMOTHY LEARY:
Because that's the only kind of trip the Establishment would let it take.

ERNEST HEMINGWAY:
To die. In the rain.

HENRY DAVID THOREAU:
To live deliberately ... to suck all the marrow out of life.

ALBERT EINSTEIN:
Whether the chicken crossed the road or the road crossed the chicken depends on your frame of reference.

WILLIAM SHAKESPEARE:
Let him not to the crossing of true roads
Admit impediments. Crossing is not crossing
Which alters when it alteration finds,
Or bends its path when roadways do intrude.

B.F. SKINNER:
A chicken who has frequently escaped an unpleasant contingency by crossing a road eventually avoids those contingencies by crossing the road before the contingency appears. Stimuli which frequently precede the contingency become reinforcers of this behavior.

JEAN-JACQUES ROUSSEAU:

As long as a chicken is constrained to stay on one side of the road, and does stay, it is acting rightly; but once that chicken is capable of shaking off its yoke and crossing the road, and does cross the road, it is acting even more rightly.

EDGAR ALLAN POE:

Deep across the roadway peering, long it
   stood there, wond'ring, fearing,
Doubting, dreaming dreams of roads no
   chickens ever crossed before,
But the roadway was unbroken, and the
   chicken gave no token
Of the fear that lay unspoken deep within
   its heart before.
Straight it plunged across the roadway, to
   the side it dreamed before,

To return, ah, nevermore.

ANDERSEN CONSULTANT:

Deregulation of the chicken's side of the road was threatening its dominant market position. The chicken was faced with significant challenges to create and develop the competencies required for the newly competitive market. Andersen Consulting, in a partnering relationship with the client, helped the chicken by rethinking its physical distribution strategy and implementation processes. Using the Poultry Integration Model (PIM), Andersen helped the chicken use its skills, methodologies, knowledge capital and experiences to align the chicken's people, processes and technology in support of its overall strategy within a Program Management framework. Andersen Consulting convened a diverse cross-spectrum of road analysts and best chickens along with Andersen consultants with deep skills in the transportation industry to engage in a two-day itinerary of meetings in order to leverage their personal knowledge capital and successfully architect and implement an enterprise-wide value framework across the continuum of poultry cross-median processes. The meeting was held in a park-like setting enabling and creating an impactful environment which was strategically based, industry-focused, and built upon a consistent, clear, and unified market message and aligned with the chicken's mission, vision, and core values. This was conducive toward the creation of a total business integration solution. Andersen Consulting helped the chicken crossing to become more successful.

When the end of the world arrives, how will the media report it?

USA Today:
WE'RE DEAD

The Wall Street Journal:
DOW JONES PLUMMETS AS WORLD ENDS

Playboy:
GIRLS OF THE APOCALYPSE

Sports Illustrated:
GAME OVER

Rolling Stone:
THE GRATEFUL DEAD REUNION TOUR

Reader's Digest:
'BYE

Discover Magazine:
HOW WILL THE EXTINCTION OF ALL LIFE AS WE KNOW IT
AFFECT THE WAY WE VIEW THE COSMOS?

TV Guide:
DEATH AND DAMNATION: NIELSEN RATINGS SOAR!

Ladies' Home Journal:
LOSE 10 LBS BY JUDGEMENT DAY WITH OUR NEW "ARMAGEDDON" DIET!

America Online:
SYSTEM TEMPORARILY DOWN. TRY CALLING BACK IN 15 MINUTES.

Inc. Magazine:
TEN WAYS YOU CAN PROFIT FROM THE APOCALYPSE

Microsoft's Web Site:
IF YOU DIDN'T EXPERIENCE THE RAPTURE,
DOWNLOAD SOFTWARE PATCH RAPT777.EXE.

Bill Gates dies in his sleep and appears before St. Peter. It's a slow day for St. Peter, and no one else happens to be around. St. Peter pulls out the Book of Life for Mr. Gates, and tells him it contains every good and bad thing he's done, no matter how small. St. Peter will be reviewing Mr. Gates's life to decide whether he goes to heaven or hell.

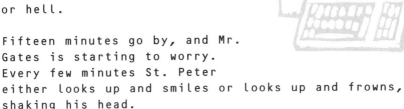

Fifteen minutes go by, and Mr. Gates is starting to worry. Every few minutes St. Peter either looks up and smiles or looks up and frowns, shaking his head.

An hour later, he closes the book and says, "You know, Bill, you brought happiness to millions of people and bettered the lives of millions more. But you are also responsible for software products which caused millions of people anguish and misery."

Pacing back and forth, St. Peter says, "I just can't decide." Then he stops and smiles. "I have an idea: I'll do something I've never done before and let you decide where you want to go."

Well, Gates is delighted. He's about to shout "Heaven!" when St. Peter interrupts and adds, "I'll let you try out each place before you decide. Which do you want to try first?"

Gates is stunned. Why would anyone pick hell? He thinks for a moment and decides that if he can go to heaven anyway, he may as well see what hell is like while he has the chance. "I'll try hell first."

St. Peter waves his arm and Gates finds himself in hell. It's warm, but not hot. There's laughter and a lot of gorgeous (scantily clad) women running around, smiling and waving to him. He hears a great band playing in the distance and sees people laughing, dancing, and having a wonderful time.

There's a flash and suddenly Gates finds himself in heaven. It's quieter than hell—no half-dressed women running around—and sleepy harp music is playing in the background. It's a peaceful setting, but not at all exciting.

There's another flash and he's back with St. Peter. "Well, which place did you prefer?"

Gates thinks about it long and hard. While heaven was nice, hell seemed a lot more fun (not to mention he thought he saw a few people he knew in hell, and he didn't recognize anyone in heaven).

"I choose hell," he says.

"Fine," says St. Peter, and with a wave of his hand Gates disappears.

Two weeks go by, and St. Peter decides to check on the billionaire. He appears in hell, and Gates is tied to a wall in a sea of boiling rock, screaming as lava laps at his feet and gargantuan creatures devour people around him.

St. Peter wanders over and asks how he's doing.

"This is nothing like the place I visited!" screams Gates.

"Oh," says St. Peter, "that was the demo."

• • •

A theory is something nobody believes, except the person who made it. An experiment is something everybody believes, except the person who made it.

• • •

Logic is a systematic method for getting the wrong conclusion...with confidence.

A MAN WHO SMELLED LIKE A DISTILLERY FLOPPED ON A SUBWAY SEAT NEXT TO A PRIEST. THE MAN'S TIE WAS STAINED, HIS FACE WAS PLASTERED WITH RED LIPSTICK, AND A HALF-EMPTY BOTTLE OF GIN WAS STICKING OUT OF HIS TORN COAT POCKET.

HE OPENED HIS NEWSPAPER AND BEGAN READING. AFTER A FEW MINUTES THE DISHEVELED GUY TURNED TO THE PRIEST AND ASKED, "SAY, FATHER, WHAT CAUSES ARTHRITIS?"

THE PRIEST, DISGUSTED BY THE MAN'S APPEARANCE AND BEHAVIOR, SNAPPED, "IT'S CAUSED BY LOOSE LIVING, BEING WITH CHEAP, WICKED WOMEN, TOO MUCH ALCOHOL, AND A CONTEMPT FOR YOUR FELLOW MAN!"

"WELL, I'LL BE," THE MAN MUTTERED, RETURNING TO HIS PAPER. THE PRIEST, THINKING ABOUT WHAT HE HAD SAID, NUDGED THE MAN AND APOLOGIZED. "I'M VERY SORRY, I DIDN'T MEAN TO COME ON SO STRONG. HOW LONG HAVE YOU HAD ARTHRITIS?"

"I DON'T HAVE IT, FATHER. I WAS JUST READING HERE THAT THE POPE DOES."

• • •

Einstein dies and goes to heaven only to be informed that his room is not yet ready.

"I hope you will not mind waiting in a dormitory. We are very sorry, but it's the best we can do and you will have to share the room with others," he is told by the doorman (say his name is Pete).

Einstein says that this is no problem at all and that there is no need to make such a great fuss. So Pete leads him to the dorm. They enter and Albert is introduced to all of the present inhabitants.

"See, here is your first roommate. He has an IQ of 180!"

"Why that's wonderful!" says Albert. "We can discuss mathematics!"

"And here is your second roommate. His IQ is 150!"
"Why, that's wonderful!" says Albert. "We can discuss physics!"

"And here is your third roommate. His IQ is 100!"

"That's wonderful! We can discuss the latest plays at the theater!"
Just then another man moves out to capture Albert's hand and shake it.

"I'm your last roommate and I'm sorry, but my IQ is only 80."

Albert smiles back at him and says, "So, where do you think interest rates are headed?"

. . .

HOLY BLOOPERS

1. This afternoon, there will be a meeting in the south and north ends of the church. Children will be baptized at both ends.

2. Tuesday at 4 p.m. there will be an ice cream social. All ladies giving milk come early.

3. Wednesday the Ladies Liturgy Society will meet. Mrs. Johnson will sing, "Put Me in My Little Bed," accompanied by the pastor.

4. Thursday at 5 p.m. there will be a meeting of the Little Mothers Club. All ladies wishing to be Little Mothers please meet with the pastor in his study.

5. This being Easter Sunday, we will ask Mrs. Johnson to come forward and lay an egg at the altar.

6. The service will close with "Little Drops of Water." One of the ladies will start quietly and the rest of the congregation will join in.

7. On Sunday, a special collection will be taken to defray the expenses of the new carpet. All those wishing to do something on the new carpet, come forward and get a piece of paper.

8. The ladies of the church have cast off clothing of every kind and they may be seen in the church basement on Friday afternoon.

9. A bean supper will be held on Saturday evening in the church basement. Music will follow.

10. The rosebud on the altar this morning is to announce the birth of David Alan Belzer, the sin of Rev. and Mrs. Belzer.

11. Tonight's sermon: "What is hell?" Come early and listen to our choir practice.

12. For those of you who have children and don't know it, we have a nursery downstairs.

13. Remember in prayer the many who are sick of our church and community.

14. Potluck supper. Prayer and medication to follow.

15. Don't let worry kill you off—let the church help.

• • •

FROM SOMEONE WITH WAY TOO MUCH TIME ON HIS HANDS...

M&M EVOLUTION

Whenever I get a package of plain M&Ms, I make it my duty to continue the strength and robustness of the candy as a species. To this end, I hold M&M duels.

Taking two candies between my thumb and forefinger, I apply pressure, squeezing them together until one of them cracks and splinters. That is the "loser," and I eat the inferior one immediately. The winner gets to go another round. I have found that, in general, the brown and red M&Ms are tougher, and the newer blue ones are genetically inferior. I have hypothesized that the blue M&Ms as a race cannot survive long in the intense theater of competition that is the modern candy and snack-food world.

Occasionally I will get a mutation, a candy that is mis-
shapen, or pointier, or flatter than the rest. Almost invari-
ably this proves to be a weakness, but on very rare occasions
it gives the candy extra strength. In this way, the species continues to adapt to its environment.

When I reach the end of the pack, I am left with one M&M,
the strongest of the herd. Since it would make no sense to
eat this one as well, I pack it neatly in an envelope and send
it to M&M Mars, A Division of Mars, Inc., Hackettstown, NJ
17840-1503 U.S.A., along with a 3x5 card reading, "Please
use this M&M for breeding purposes."

This week they wrote back to thank me, and sent me a coupon
for a free 1/2 pound bag of plain M&Ms. I consider this
"grant money." I have set aside the weekend for a grand tournament. From a field of hundreds, I will discover the True
Champion.

There can be only one.

THE UNIVERSE

DOUGLAS ADAMS: "There is a theory which states that if ever anybody discovers exactly what the Universe is for and why it is here, it will instantly disappear and be replaced by something even more bizarre and inexplicable. There is another theory which states that this has already happened."

ALBERT EINSTEIN: "Only two things are infinite, the universe and human stupidity, and I'm not sure about the former."

EDWARD P. TRYON: "In answer to the question of why it happened, I offer the modest proposal that our Universe is simply one of those things which happen from time to time."

MAX FRISCH: "Technology is a way of organizing the universe so that man doesn't have to experience it."

FRED HOYLE: "There is a coherent plan in the universe, though I don't know what it's a plan for."

CHRISTOPHER MORLEY: "My theology, briefly, is that the universe was dictated but not signed."

The local bar was so sure that its bartender was the strongest man around that it offered a standing $1,000 bet.

The bartender would squeeze a lemon until all the juice ran into a glass, and hand the lemon to a patron. Anyone who could squeeze out one more drop of juice would win the money.

Many people had tried over time (weight lifters, longshoremen, etc.), but nobody could do it.

One day this scrawny little man came into the bar, wearing thick glasses and a polyester suit, and said in a tiny, squeaky voice, "I'd like to try the bet."

After the laughter had died down, the bartender said OK, grabbed a lemon, and squeezed away. Then he handed the wrinkled remains of the rind to the little man.

But the crowd's laughter turned to total silence as the man clenched his fist around the lemon and six drops fell into the glass.

As the crowd cheered, the bartender paid the $1,000 and asked the little man, "What do you do for a living? Are you a lumberjack, a weight lifter, or what?"

The man replied, "I work for the IRS."

VOTE DEMOCRAT–
IT'S EASIER THAN WORKING !!!

VOTE REPUBLICAN–
IT'S EASIER THAN THINKING !!!

...

POLITICS: IT ALL REALLY JUST BOILS DOWN TO THIS:

CRIMINALS
Democrats: Give them a second chance.
Republicans: Give them the swift sword of death.

THE POOR
Democrats: Give them some food.
Republicans: Give them the swift sword
of death.

ENDANGERED SPECIES
Democrats: Give them protection.
Republicans: Give them the swift sword
of death.

DICTATORS
Democrats: Give them a way out.
Republicans: Give them the swift sword
of death.

THE UNINSURED
Democrats: Give them health care.
Republicans: Give them the swift sword
of death.

*THE COST
Democrats: $9,000,000,000,000,000,000
Republicans: $29.95 (cost of one sword)

STILL PICKIN' ON THE IRISH

NE DAY AN Englishman, a Scotsman, and an Irishman walked into a pub together. They proceeded to each buy a pint of Guinness. Just as they were about to enjoy their creamy beverage three flies landed in each of their pints, and were stuck in the thick head.

The Englishman pushed his beer away from him in disgust.

The Scotsman fished the offending fly out of his beer and continued drinking it as if nothing had happened.

The Irishman, too, picked the fly out of his drink, held it out over the beer and then started yelling, "SPIT IT OUT, SPIT IT OUT, YA BASTARD!!!!"

• • •

An Irishman walks into a bar in Dublin, orders three pints of Guinness and sits in the back of the room drinking a sip out of each one in turn. When he finishes them he comes back to the bar and orders three more. The bartender says to him:

"You know, a pint starts going flat after I draw it. It would taste better if you bought one pint at a time."

The Irishman replies, "Well you see I have two brothers. One is in America, the other in Australia, and I'm here in Dublin. When we all left home we promised that we'd drink this way to remember the days when we drank together." The bartender is touched at this nice custom and leaves it there.

The Irishman becomes a regular in the bar and always drinks the same way: He orders three pints and drinks them in turn. One day he comes in and orders two pints. All the other regulars notice and fall silent. When he comes back to the bar for the second round, the bartender says, "I don't want to intrude on your grief, but I wanted to offer my condolences on your great loss."

The Irishman looks confused for a moment, then a light dawns in his eye and he laughs. "Oh no," he says, "everyone's fine. I've just quit drinking."

Work
& School

Management
Appreciation

THE SAGA OF MANAGEMENT REVIEW OF WRITING STYLE

QUESTION: How many feet do mice have?

ORIGINAL REPLY: Mice have four feet.
Mgmt comment: Elaborate.

REVISION 1:   Mice have five appendages, four of
                     which are feet.
Mgmt comment: No discussion of fifth appendage.

REVISION 2:   Mice have five appendages; four of
                     them are feet and one is a tail.
Mgmt comment: What? Feet with no legs?

REVISION 3:   Mice have four legs, four feet, and
                     one tail per unit-mouse.
Mgmt comment: Confusing. Is that a total of 9 appendages?

REVISION 4:   Mice have four leg-foot assemblies
                   and one tail assembly per body.

Mgmt comment: Does not fully discuss the issue.

REVISION 5:   Each mouse comes equipped with four
                   legs and a tail. Each leg is equipped
                   with a foot at the end opposite the
                   body; the tail is not equipped with a foot.

Mgmt comment: Descriptive but not decisive.

REVISION 6:   Allotment appendages for mice will be:
                   FOUR LEG-FOOT ASSEMBLIES, ONE TAIL.
                   Deviation from this policy is not
                   permitted as it would constitute
                   misapportionment of scarce appendage
                   assets.

Mgmt comment: Too authoritative; stifles creativity.

REVISION 7:   Mice have four feet; each foot is
                   attached to a small leg joined integrally
                   with the overall mouse structural
                   sub-system. Also attached to the
                   mouse sub-system is a thin tail,
                   non-functional and ornamental in nature.

Mgmt comment: Too verbose/scientific.
                   Answer the question.

FINAL REVISION: Mice have four feet.

Mgmt comment: Approved.

PRISON VS. WORK

In prison you spend a majority of your time in an 8x10 cell. At work you spend most of your time in a 6x8 cubicle.

In prison you get three meals a day. At work you only get a break for one meal and you have to pay for that one.

In prison you get time off for good behavior. At work you get rewarded for good behavior with more work.

At work you must carry a security card and unlock and open all the doors yourself. In prison a guard locks and unlocks all the doors for you.

In prison you can watch TV and play games. At work you get fired for watching TV and playing games.

In prison you get your own toilet. At work you have to share.

In prison they allow your family and friends to visit. At work you can't even speak to your family and friends.

In prison all expenses are paid by taxpayers with no work required. At work you get to pay all the expenses to go to work and then they deduct taxes from your salary to pay for prisoners.

In prison there are sadistic wardens. At work you have managers.

NOTICE TO ALL EMPLOYEES:

It has come to our attention recently that many of you have been turning in timesheets that specify large amounts of "Miscellaneous Unproductive Time" (code 5309). To our department, unproductive time isn't a problem. What is a problem, however, is not knowing exactly what you are doing during your unproductive time.

Attached below is a sheet specifying a tentative extended job code list based on our observations of employee activities. The list will allow you to specify with a fair amount of precision what you are doing during your unproductive time. Please begin using this job code list immediately and let us know about any difficulties you encounter.

Thank you,

The Management

Attached: Extended Job Code List

Code #	Explanation
5316	Meeting
5318	Trying to Sound Knowledgeable While in Meeting
5319	Waiting for Break
5320	Waiting for Lunch
5321	Waiting for End of Day
5393	Covering for Incompetence of Coworker
5400	Trying to Explain Concept to Coworker Who Is Not Interested in Learning
5401	Trying to Explain Concept to Coworker Who Is Stupid
5402	Trying to Explain Concept to Coworker Who Hates You

5481	Buying Snack
5482	Eating Snack
5500	Filling Out Timesheet
5501	Inventing Timesheet Entries
5502	Waiting for Something to Happen
5503	Scratching Yourself
5504	Sleeping
5510	Feeling Bored
5511	Feeling Horny
5600	Griping About Lousy Job
5601	Griping About Low Pay
5602	Griping About Long Hours
5603	Griping About Coworker
5604	Griping About Boss
5605	Griping About Personal Problems
5640	Miscellaneous Unproductive Griping
5701	Not Actually Present at Job
6200	Using Company Resources for Personal Profit
6201	Stealing Company Goods
6203	Using Company Phone to Make Long-Distance Personal Calls
6204	Using Company Phone to Make Long-Distance Personal Calls in Order to Sell Stolen Company Goods
6206	Gossip
6207	Planning a Social Event
6221	Pretending to Work While Boss Is Watching
6222	Pretending to Enjoy Your Job
6611	Staring into Space
6612	Staring at Computer Screen
6615	Transcendental Meditation
7281	Extended Visit to the Bathroom

ELEMENT DISCOVERED

Washington, D.C., Jan. 21—The heaviest element known to science was discovered recently by physicists at the Naval Research Laboratory in Washington DC. The element—tentatively named Administratium—has no protons or electrons and thus has an atomic number of 0. However it does have 1 neutron, 125 assistant neutrons, 75 vice neutrons, and 111 assistant vice neutrons. This gives it an atomic mass of 312. These 312 particles are held together in a nucleus by a force that involves the continuous exchange of meson-like particles called morons.

Since it has no electrons, Administratium is inert. However it can be detected chemically as it impedes every reaction it comes in contact with. According to the discoverers, a minute amount of Administratium caused one reaction to take over four days to complete when it would normally occur in less than one second.

Administratium has a normal half-life of approximately 3 years, at which time it does not actually decay but instead undergoes a reorganization in which assistant neutrons, vice neutrons, and assistant vice neutrons change places. Some studies have shown that the atomic weight actually increases after each reorganization.

Research at other laboratories indicates that Administratium occurs naturally in the atmosphere. It tends to concentrate at certain points such as government agencies, large corporations, universities and the United Nations. It can actually be found in the newest, best maintained buildings.

Scientists point out that Administratium is known to be toxic at any level of concentration and can easily destroy any positive reactions where it is allowed to accumulate. Attempts are being made to determine how Administratium can be controlled to prevent irreversible damage, but results to date are not promising.

Engineers (& Other Techies)

Three men—a physicist, an engineer and a computer scientist—are traveling in a car. Suddenly, the car starts smoking and the engine stops. The three worried men try to solve the problem.

The physicist says, "This is obviously a classic problem of torque. It has overloaded the elasticity limit of the main axis."

The engineer says, "Let's be serious! The matter is that it has burned the spark of the connecting rod to the dynamo of the radiator. I can easily repair it by hammering."

The computer scientist says, "What if we get out of the car, wait a minute, then get in and try again?"

• • •

A statistician can have his head under a sun lamp and his feet in ice, and say that on the average he feels fine.

The hardware engineer, software engineer, and project manager went out for a walk at lunch when they stumbled across an ancient-looking lamp sticking out of the ground. The three engineers pried the lamp out of the ground and were dusting it off when a genie appeared in a cloud of smoke before them.

"For freeing me from my prison I shall grant you the customary three wishes!" says the genie. "Since there are three of you, I grant you each one wish."

The software engineer blurts out, "I want to spend my life riding my Harley through the Southwest with a beautiful woman behind me!"

"It shall be so!" says the genie, and the engineer disappears with a poof.

The hardware engineer says, "That's a great idea. I want to be sailing through the South Pacific on a magnificent sailboat with an all-female crew."

"So it shall be!" says the genie, and he, too, disappears with a poof.

The genie then turns to the project manager and says, "You have the last wish!"

The manager looks at where his engineers were standing and says, "I'd like to have those guys back at their desks after lunch."

Doctors & Lawyers

Four surgeons are taking a coffee break and discussing their work.

The first one says, "I think accountants are the easiest to operate on. Everything inside is numbered."

"I think librarians are the easiest," says the second surgeon. "When you open them up all their organs are alphabetically ordered."

The third surgeon says, "I prefer to operate on electricians. All their organs are color coded."

The fourth one says, "I like to operate on lawyers. They're heartless, spineless, and gutless, and their heads and behinds are interchangeable."

• • •

One day, a man is walking along the beach and comes across an odd-looking bottle. Not being one to ignore tradition, he rubs it and, much to his surprise, a genie actually appears.

"For releasing me from the bottle, I will grant you three wishes," says the genie.

The man is ecstatic. "But there's a catch," the genie continues.

"What catch?" asks the man, eyeing the genie suspiciously.

The genie replies, "For each of your wishes, every lawyer in the world will receive DOUBLE what you ask for."

"Hey, I can live with that! No problem!" replies the elated man.

"What is your first wish?" asks the genie.

"Well, I've always wanted a Ferrari!"

POOF! A Ferrari appears in front of the man. "Now, every lawyer in the world has been given TWO Ferraris," says the genie.

"What is your next wish?"

"I could really use a million dollars," replies the man, and POOF! One million dollars appears at his feet. "Now, every lawyer in the world is TWO million dollars richer," the genie reminds the man.

"Well, that's okay, as long as I've got MY million," replies the man.

"And what is your final wish?" asks the genie.

The man thinks long and hard, and finally says, "Well, you know, I've always wanted to donate a kidney."

• • •

Q. I just joined a new HMO. How difficult will it be to choose the doctor I want?

A. Just slightly more difficult than choosing your parents. Your insurer will provide you with a book listing all the doctors who were participating in the plan at the time the information was gathered. These doctors basically fall into two categories—those who are no longer accepting new patients, and those who will see you but are no longer part of the plan. But don't worry—the remaining doctor who is still in the plan and accepting new patients has an office just a half day's drive away!

Q. What are pre-existing conditions?

A. This is a phrase used by the grammatically challenged when they want to talk about existing conditions. Unfortunately, we appear to be pre-stuck with it.

Q. Well, can I get coverage for my pre-existing conditions?

A. Certainly, as long as they don't require any treatment.

Q. What happens if I want to try alternative forms of medicine?

A. You'll need to find alternative forms of payment.

Q. My pharmacy plan only covers generic drugs, but I need the name brand. I tried the generic medication, but it gave me a stomachache. What should I do?

A. Poke yourself in the eye.

Computerland

**THE TOP 12 THINGS YOU DON'T
WANT TO HEAR FROM TECH SUPPORT**

12. "Do you have a sledgehammer or a brick handy?"

11. "…that's right, not even McGyver could fix it."

10. "So, what are you wearing?"

9. "Duuuuuude! Bummer!"

8. "Looks like you're gonna need some new dilithium crystals, Cap'n."

7. "Press 1 for Support. Press 2 if you're with 60 Minutes.
Press 3 if you're with the FTC."

6. "We can fix this, but you're gonna need a butter knife,
a roll of duct tape, and a car battery."

5. "I'm sorry, Dave. I'm afraid I can't do that."

4.   "In layman's terms, we call that the Hindenburg Effect."

3.   "Hold on a second ...Mom! Timmy's hitting me!"

2.   "Okay, turn to page 523 in your copy of Dianetics."

and the Number 1 Thing You Don't Want to Hear From Tech Support...

1.   "PLEASE HOLD FOR MR. GATES'S ATTORNEY."

• • •

ALPHA GEEK
The most knowledgeable, technically proficient person in an office or work group. "Ask Larry, he's the alpha geek around here."

BEEPILEPSY
The brief seizure people sometimes suffer when their beepers go off, especially in vibrator mode. Characterized by physical spasms, goofy facial expressions, and stopping speech in mid-sentence.

BOOKMARK
To take note of a person for future reference (a metaphor borrowed from web browsers). "I bookmarked him after seeing his cool demo at Siggraph."

DEAD TREE EDITION
The paper version of a publication available in both paper and electronic forms, as in: "The dead tree edition of the San Francisco Chronicle."

EGOSURFING
Scanning the net, databases, print media, or research papers looking for the mention of your name.

404
Someone who's clueless. From the World Wide Web message "404, URL Not Found," meaning that the document you've tried to access can't be located. "Don't bother asking him ... he's 404, man."

GLAZING

Corporate-speak for sleeping with your eyes open. A popular pastime at conferences and early morning meetings. "Didn't you notice that half the room was glazing by the second session?"

GRAYBAR LAND

The place you go while you're staring at a computer that's processing something very slowly (while you watch the gray bar creep across the screen). "I was in graybar land for what seemed like hours, thanks to that CAD rendering."

KEYBOARD PLAQUE

The disgusting buildup of dirt and crud found on computer keyboards. "Are there any other terminals I can use? This one has a bad case of keyboard plaque."

OPEN-COLLAR WORKERS

People who work at home or telecommute.

PLUG-AND-PLAY

A new hire who doesn't need any training. "The new guy, John, is great. He's totally plug-and-play."

WORLD WIDE WAIT

The real meaning of WWW.

• • •

COMPUTER PROBLEM REPORT FORM

1. Describe your problem:
_____

2. Now describe the problem accurately:
_____

3. Speculate wildly about the cause of the problem:
_____

4. Problem Severity:
   A. Minor _____   B. Minor _____
   C. Minor _____   D. Trivial ___

5. Is your computer plugged in? Yes_ No_

6. Is it turned on? Yes_ No_

7. Have you tried to fix it yourself? Yes_ No_

8. Have you made it worse? Yes_

9. Have you read the manual? Yes_ No_

10. Are you sure you've read the manual? Yes_ No_

11. Are you absolutely certain you've read the manual? No_

12. Do you think you understood it? Yes_ No_

13. If "Yes" then why can't you fix the problem yourself?
_____

14. How tall are you? Are you above this line?_____

15. What were you doing with your computer at the time the
problem occurred? _____

16. If "nothing" explain why you were logged in.
_____

17. Are you sure you aren't imagining the problem? Yes_ No_

18. How does this problem make you feel?_____

19. Tell me about your childhood._____

20. Do you have any independent witnesses of the problem?
Yes_ No_

21. Can't you do something else instead of bothering me?
Yes__

The graduate with a Science degree asks,

"Why does it work?"

The graduate with an Engineering degree asks,

"How does it work?"

The graduate with an Accounting degree asks,

"How much will it cost?"

The graduate with a Liberal Arts degree asks,

"Do you want ~~mustard~~ with that?"

 ...

Q: How many PRINCETON students does it take to change a lightbulb?
A: Two—one to mix the martinis and one to call the electrician.

Q: How many COLUMBIA students does it take to change a lightbulb?
A: Seventy-six—one to change the lightbulb, 50 to protect the lightbulb's right to change, and 25 to hold a counter-protest.

Q: How many YALE students does it take to change a lightbulb?
A: None—New Haven looks better in the dark.

Q. How many ~~HARVARD~~ students does it take to change a lightbulb?
A: One—he holds the bulb and the world revolves around him.

Q: How many MIT students does it take to change a lightbulb?
A: Five—one to design a nuclear-powered one that never needs changing, one to figure out how to power Boston using the nuked lightbulb, two to install it, and one to write the computer program that controls the wall switch.

Q: How many STANFORD students does it take to change a lightbulb?
A: One, dude.

Q: How many DUKE students does it take to change a lightbulb?
A: A whole frat—but only one of them is sober enough to get the bulb out of the socket.

RECEIVED FROM AN ENGLISH PROFESSOR
This assignment was actually turned in by two English students:

In-class Assignment for Wednesday
Today we will experiment with a new form called the tandem story. The process is simple. Each person will pair off with the person sitting to his or her immediate right. One of you will then write the first paragraph of a short story. The partner will read the first paragraph and then add another paragraph to the story. The first person will then add a third paragraph and so on back and forth. Remember to reread what has been written each time in order to keep the story coherent. The story is over when both agree a conclusion has been reached.

At first, Laurie couldn't decide which kind of tea she wanted. The camomile which used to be her favorite for lazy evenings at home now reminded her too much of Carl who once said in happier times that he liked camomile. But she felt she must now at all costs keep her mind off Carl. His possessiveness was suffocating and if she thought about him too much her asthma started acting up again. So camomile was out of the question.

Meanwhile, Advance Sergeant Carl Harris, leader of the attack squadron now in orbit over Skylon 4, had more important things to think about than the neuroses of an air-headed asthmatic bimbo named Laurie with whom he had spent one sweaty night over a year ago. "A.S. Harris to Geostation 17," he said into his transgalactic communicator. "Polar orbit established. No sign of resistance so far...." But before he could sign off a bluish particle beam flashed out of nowhere and blasted a hole through his ship's cargo bay. The jolt from the direct hit sent him flying out of his seat and across the cockpit.

He bumped his head and died almost immediately but not before he felt one last pang of regret for psychically brutalizing the one woman who had ever had feelings for him. Soon afterwards Earth stopped its pointless hostilities toward the peaceful farmers of Skylon 4. "Congress Passes Law Permanently Abolishing War and Space Travel" Laurie read in her newspaper one morning. The news simultaneously excited her and bored her. She stared out the window dreaming of her youth—when the days had passed unhurriedly and carefree with no newspapers to read, no television to distract her from her sense of innocent wonder at all the beautiful things around her. "Why must one lose one's innocence to become a woman?" she pondered wistfully.

Little did she know she had less than 10 seconds to live. Thousands of miles above the city, the Anu'udrian mothership launched the first of its lithium fusion missiles. The dim-witted wimpy peaceniks who pushed the Unilateral Aerospace Disarmament Treaty through Congress had left Earth a defenseless target for the hostile alien empires who were determined to destroy the human race. Within two hours after the passage of the treaty the Anu'udrian ships were on course for Earth carrying enough firepower to pulverize the entire planet. With no one to stop them they swiftly initiated their diabolical plan. The lithium fusion missile entered the atmosphere unimpeded. The President, in his top-secret mobile submarine headquarters on the ocean floor off the coast of Guam, felt the inconceivably massive explosion which vaporized Laurie and 85 million other Americans. The President slammed his fist on the conference table. "We can't allow this! I'm going to veto that treaty! Let's blow 'em out of the sky!"

This is absurd. I refuse to continue this mockery of literature. My writing partner is a violent, chauvinistic, semiliterate adolescent.

Yeah? Well you're a self-centered, tedious neurotic whose attempts at writing are the literary equivalent of Valium.

Jerk.

Jerk.

A true story. A thermodynamics professor had written a take-home exam for his graduate students. It had one question:

Is hell exothermic or endothermic?
Support your answer with a proof.

Most of the students wrote proofs of their beliefs using Boyle's Law or some variant. One student, however, wrote the following:

"First, we postulate that if souls exist, then they must have some mass.

If they do, then a mole of souls can also have a mass. So, at what rate are souls moving into hell and at what rate are souls leaving? I think we can safely assume that once a soul gets to hell, it will not leave. Therefore, no souls are leaving.

As for souls entering hell, let's look at the different religions that exist in the world today. Some of these religions state that if you are not a member of their religion, you will go to hell.

Since there are more than one of these religions and people do not belong to more than one religion, we can project that all people and all souls go to hell.

With birth and death rates as they are, we can expect the number of souls in hell to increase exponentially.

Now, we look at the rate of change in volume in hell. Boyle's Law states that in order for the temperature and pressure in hell to stay the same, the ratio of the mass of souls and volume needs to stay constant.

So, if hell is expanding at a slower rate than the rate at which souls enter hell, then the temperature and pressure in hell will increase until all hell breaks loose.

Of course, if hell is expanding at a rate faster than the increase of souls in hell, then the temperature and pressure will drop until hell freezes over."

It was not revealed what grade the student received.

Language

AQUADEXTROUS (ak wa deks' trus) *adj.* Possessing the ability to turn the bathtub faucet on and off with your toes.

AQUALIBRIUM (ak wa lib' re um) *n.* The point where the stream of drinking fountain water is at its perfect height, thus relieving the drinker from (a) having to suck the nozzle, or (b) squirting himself in the eye.

BURGACIDE (burg' uh side) *n.* When a hamburger can't take any more torture and hurls itself through the grill into the coals.

CARPERPETUATION (kar' pur pet u a shun) *n.* The act, when vacuuming, of running over a string or a piece of lint at least a dozen times, reaching over and picking it up, examining it, then putting it back down to give the vacuum one more chance.

DISCONFECT (dis kon fekt') *v.* To sterilize the piece of candy you dropped on the floor by blowing on it, somehow assuming this will "remove" all the germs.

ECNALUBMA (ek na lub' ma) *n.* A rescue vehicle which can only be seen in the rearview mirror.

EIFFELITES (eye' ful eyetz) *n.* Gangly people sitting in front of you at the movies who, no matter what direction you lean in, follow suit.

ELBONICS (el bon' iks) *n.* The actions of two people maneuvering for one armrest in a movie theater.

ELECELLERATION (el a cel er ay' shun) *n.* The mistaken notion that the more you press an elevator button the faster the elevator will arrive.

FRUST (frust) *n.* The small line of debris that refuses to be swept onto the dust pan and keeps backing a person across the room until he finally decides to give up and sweep it under the rug.

LACTOMANGULATION (lak' to man gyu lay' shun) *n.* Manhandling the "open here" spout on a milk container so badly that one has to resort to the "illegal" side.

NEONPHANCY (ne on' fan see) *n.* A fluorescent light bulb struggling to come to life.

PEPPIER (pehp ee ay') *n.* The waiter at a fancy restaurant whose sole purpose seems to be walking around asking diners if they want ground pepper.

PHONESIA (fo nee' zhuh) *n.* The affliction of dialing a phone number and forgetting whom you were calling just as they answer.

PUPKUS (pup' kus) *n.* The moist residue left on a window after a dog presses its nose to it.

TELECRASTINATION (tel e kras tin ay' shun) *n.* The act of always letting the phone ring at least twice before you pick it up, even when you're only six inches away.

• • •

THE IMPORTANCE OF PUNCTUATION

Dear John,
I want a man who knows what love is all about. You are generous, kind, thoughtful. People who are not like you admit to being useless and inferior. You have ruined me for other men. I yearn for you. I have no feelings whatsoever when we're apart. I can be forever happy — will you let me be yours?

Gloria

Dear John,
I want a man who knows what love is. All about you are generous, kind, thoughtful people, who are not like you. Admit to being useless and inferior. You have ruined me. For other men, I yearn. For you, I have no feelings whatsoever. When we're apart, I can be forever happy. Will you let me be?

Yours,
Gloria

FOOD FOR THOUGHT

- Is there another word for *synonym?*
- Isn't it a bit unnerving that doctors call what they do "practice"?
- When sign makers go on strike, is anything written on their signs?
- When you open a bag of cotton balls, is the top one meant to be thrown away?
- Where do forest rangers go to "get away from it all"?
- Why isn't there mouse-flavored cat food?
- Why do they report power outages on TV?
- What do you do when you see an endangered animal that is eating an endangered plant?
- Is it possible to be totally partial?
- What's another word for *thesaurus?*
- If a parsley farmer is sued, can they garnish his wages?
- When it rains, why don't sheep shrink?
- Should vegetarians eat animal crackers?
- If the police arrest a mime, do they tell him he has the right to remain silent?
- Why is the word *abbreviation* so long?
- When companies ship styrofoam, what do they pack it in?
- If vegetable oil is made out of vegetables, what is baby oil made out of?

• • •

HANDY SHAKESPEAREAN INSULT GUIDE

Combine one word from each of the three columns below and preface with "Thou."
Repeat as necessary.

Column 1	Column 2	Column 3
artless	base-court	apple-john
bawdy	bat-fowling	baggage
beslubbering	beef-witted	barnacle
bootless	beetle-headed	bladder
churlish	boil-brained	boar-pig
cockered	clapper-clawed	bugbear
clouted	clay-brained	bum-bailey
craven	common-kissing	canker-blossom

currish	crook-pated	clack-dish
dankish	dismal-dreaming	clotpole
dissembling	dizzy-eyed	coxcomb
droning	doghearted	codpiece
errant	dread-bolted	death-token
fawning	earth-vexing	dewberry
fobbing	elf-skinned	flap-dragon
froward	fat-kidneyed	flax-wench
frothy	fen-sucked	flirt-gill
gleeking	flap-mouthed	foot-licker
goatish	fly-bitten	fustilarian
gorbellied	folly-fallen	giglet
impertinent	fool-born	gudgeon
infectious	full-gorged	haggard
jarring	guts-griping	harpy
loggerheaded	half-faced	hedge-pig
lumpish	hasty-witted	horn-beast
mammering	hedge-born	hugger-mugger
mangled	hell-hated	jointhead
mewling	idle-headed	lewdster
paunchy	ill-breeding	lout
pribbling	ill-nurtured	maggot-pie
puking	knotty-pated	malt-worm
puny	milk-livered	mammet
qualling	motley-minded	measle
rank	onion-eyed	minnow
reeky	plume-plucked	miscreant
roguish	pottle-deep	moldwarp
ruttish	pox-marked	mumble-news
saucy	reeling-ripe	ut-hook
spleeny	rough-hewn	pigeon-egg
spongy	rude-growing	pignut
surly	rump-fed	puttock
tottering	shard-borne	pumpion
unmuzzled	sheep-biting	ratsbane
vain	spur-galled	scut
venomed	swag-bellied	skainsmate
villainous	tardy-gaited	strumpet
warped	tickle-brained	varlot
wayward	toad-spotted	vassal
weedy	urchin-snouted	whey-face
yeasty	weather-bitten	wagtail

Guys Only

Guy Etiquette

HERE'S A TEST:

Men should ace this test...women may have a little difficulty.

There IS a code of "Restroom Etiquette" that MUST be followed.

The following is the urinal configuration in a sample men's room.

An X above the number will indicate "in use."

(Sample):

| | |x| | |x|

(Indicates that urinals 3 and 6 are occupied.)

| 1 | 2 | 3 | 4 | 5 | 6 |

• • •

You are to identify correctly, based on urinal etiquette, at which stall you should stand.

GOOD LUCK!

EASY SECTION

1.

| | |x| |x| | |
(Urinals 2 and 4 occupied.)

| 1 | 2 | 3 | 4 | 5 | 6 |

Your choice: ___

Correct answer: 6
It's the ONLY one to go to and every guy instinctively knows this.

2.

|x| | | | | |
(Urinal 1 occupied.)

| 1 | 2 | 3 | 4 | 5 | 6 |

Your choice: ___

Correct answer: 6
Stall 5 is acceptable, but you run a greater risk of being next to someone who arrives later.

KIND OF TRICKY SECTION

3.

| | | | | | |
(empty)

| 1 | 2 | 3 | 4 | 5 | 6 |

Your choice: __

Correct answer: 1 or 6
You are tacitly saying, "I don't want anyone next to me."

4.

| | |x| |x| |x|
(2, 4 and 6 occupied)

| 1 | 2 | 3 | 4 | 5 | 6 |

Your choice: ___

Correct answer: 1
You're stuck being next to at least ONE guy, so you minimize the impact and get a wall on your left. NEVER go between TWO guys if you can help it. Exceptions to this are stadium restrooms where the herd thunders in.

SUBTLE, TRICKY, BUT IMPORTANT TO KNOW SECTION

5.

| | |x| | |x|x|
(2, 5 and 6 occupied)

| 1 | 2 | 3 | 4 | 5 | 6 |

Your choice: __

Correct answer: 4

Believe it or not, 1 and 3 "couples" you with the guy in stall 2. And we wouldn't want THAT now, would we? This differs from question 4 in such a subtle way that the nuances cannot be explained. Suffice it to say, only men would understand!

VERY TRICKY INDEED SECTION

6.

| x | x | | | | x | x |

(1, 2, 5 and 6 occupied)

| 1 | 2 | 3 | 4 | 5 | 6 |

Your choice: ___

Correct answer: NONE!
You go to the mirror and pretend to comb your hair or straighten a tie until the urinals "open up" a bit more. If you have to go REAL, REAL BAD, for God's sake, use a doored stall.

OTHER PARTS OF THE
UNWRITTEN CODE OF THE URINALS

- NO talking, unless it's a good friend. But even then, keep it terse and unemotional. This ain't no clubhouse.

- I don't think I need to tell you, absolutely NO touching of anyone other than yourself. A touch of another's elbow is of the highest offense.

- NO singing. Period.

- Glances are for purposes of acknowledgment only: "Yeah, I see you there. I will not look again."

MEN'S 20 OR SO RULES FOR WOMEN

by Every Guy in America

1. It is only common courtesy that you should leave the seat on the toilet UP when you are done.

2. If you are cooking a special dinner for a man, be sure to include something from each of the four major male food groups: Meat, Fried, Beer, and Red.

3. Don't make him hold your purse in the mall.

4. The man is ALWAYS in charge of poking the campfire with a stick and/or tending the grill.

5. Any attempt by a man to prepare food no matter how feeble (i.e., microwaving a burrito, fixing spaghetti, etc.) should be met with roughly the same degree of praise that a parent might shower upon an infant when it walks for the first time.

6. Those male models with perfect bodies are all gay. Accept it.

7. Of COURSE he wants another beer.

8. Any sort of injury involving the testicles is not funny.

9. If he has to sit through "Legends of the Fall," you have to sit through "Showgirls."

10. Do not question a man's innate navigational abilities by suggesting he stop for directions.

11. He was not looking at that other girl.

12. Well, okay, maybe a little.

13. Okay, so what! He was looking at her. Big deal. Like you've never looked at another guy....

14. He is the funniest, strongest, best-looking, most successful man you have ever met.

15. And all your friends think so too, especially the cute ones.

16. Your (select appropriate item: legs/butt/hair/makeup) look(s) fine. As a matter of fact it/they look damn good. Stop asking.

17. Dirty laundry comes in several categories:
    Looks fine/smells fine
    Looks fine/smells bad
    Looks dirty/smells fine.

    Unless you intend to wash it, do not try to disrupt piles organized in this manner.

18. Yes, Sharon Stone/Pamela Anderson/Cindy Crawford is prettier than you. Just like Brad Pitt/AntonioBanderas/Keanu Reeves is better looking than him. But since neither one of you is going to be dating any of these people, love the one you're with.

19. Of course size matters, and boy does he have the grandaddy of them all.

20. His (fill in appropriate selection: bald spot/beer gut/back hair) is cute.

A small town farmer had three daughters. Being a single father, he tended to be a little overprotective of his daughters. When gentlemen came to take his daughters out on a date, he would greet them with a shotgun to make sure they knew who was boss. One evening, all of his daughters were going out on dates. The doorbell rang, the farmer got his shotgun, and answered the door. A gentleman said,

Hi, I'm Joe,
I'm here for Flo,
We're goin' to the show,
Is she ready to go?

The farmer frowned but decided to let them go. The doorbell rang again, the farmer got his shotgun, and answered the door. A gentleman said,

Hi, I'm Eddie,
I'm here for Betty,
We're gettin' spaghetti,
Is she ready?

The farmer frowned but decided to let them go. The doorbell rang again, the farmer got his shotgun, and answered the door. A gentleman said,

Hi, I'm Rex...

And the farmer shot him.

There are these three guys and they're out having a relaxing day fishing. Out of the blue they catch a mermaid who begs to be set free in return for granting each of them a wish.

Now one of the guys just doesn't believe it and says, "OK, if you can really grant wishes, then double my I.Q."

The mermaid says, "Done." Suddenly the guy starts reciting Shakespeare flawlessly and analyzing it with extreme insight.

The second guy is so amazed he says to the mermaid, "Triple my I.Q." The mermaid says, "Done." The guy starts to spout out all the mathematical solutions to problems that have been stumping scientists of varying fields for decades.

The last guy is so enthralled with the changes in his friends that he says to the mermaid, "Quintuple my I.Q." The mermaid looks at him and says, "You know, I normally don't try to change people's minds when they make a wish, but I really wish you'd reconsider."

The guy says, "Nope. I want you to increase my I.Q. by a factor of five, and if you don't do it I won't set you free."

"Please," says the mermaid, "you don't know what you're asking...it will change your entire view on the universe. Won't you ask for something else? A million dollars? Anything?"

But no matter what the mermaid said, the guy insisted on having his I.Q. increased by five times its usual power.

So the mermaid sighed and said,
"Done."
And she turned him into a woman.

The
Family Zone
(Sort of)

BUMPER STICKERS FROM AROUND THE U.S.:

I love animals! They taste great!

EARTH FIRST! We'll strip-mine the other planets later.

A flashlight is a case for holding dead batteries.

Lottery: A tax on people who are bad at math.

Hard work has a future payoff. **Laziness pays off now.**

Where there's a will, I want to be in it.

Warning: Dates in calendar are closer than they appear.

Give me ambiguity or give me something else.

We are born naked, wet and hungry. Then things get worse.

Make it idiot-proof and someone will make a better idiot.

Always remember you're unique, just like everyone else.

"Very funny, Scotty. Now beam down my clothes."

Change is inevitable, except from a vending machine.

Agroup of chess enthusiasts had checked into a hotel, and were standing in the lobby discussing their recent tournament victories. After about an hour, the manager came out of the office and asked them to disperse. "But why?" they asked as they moved off. "Because," he said, "I can't stand chess nuts boasting in an open foyer."

• • •

A doctor made it his regular habit to stop off at a bar for a hazelnut daiquiri on his way home. The bartender knew of his habit, and would always have the drink waiting at precisely 5:03 p.m. One afternoon, as the end of the workday approached, the bartender was dismayed to find that he was out of hazelnut extract. Thinking quickly, he threw together a daiquiri made with hickory nuts and set it on the bar. The doctor came in at his regular time, took one sip of the drink and exclaimed, "This isn't a hazelnut daiquiri!" "No, I'm sorry," replied the bartender, "it's a hickory daiquiri, doc."

• • •

A guy goes to a psychiatrist. "Doc, I keep having these alternating recurring dreams. First I'm a teepee; then I'm a wigwam; then I'm a teepee; then I'm a wigwam. It's driving me crazy. What's wrong with me?" The doctor replies, "It's very simple. You're two tents."

• • •

A man goes to his dentist because he feels something wrong in his mouth. The dentist examines him and says, "That new upper plate I put in for you six months ago is eroding. What have you been eating?" The man replies, "All I can think of is that about four months ago my wife made some asparagus and put some stuff on it that was delicious: hollandaise sauce. I loved it so much I put it on everything now—meat, toast, fish, vegetables, everything!" "Well," says the dentist, "that's probably the problem. Hollandaise sauce is made with lots of lemon juice, which is highly corrosive. It's eaten away your upper plate. I'll make you a new plate, and this time I'll use chrome." "Why chrome?" asks the patient. To which the dentist replies, "It's simple. Everyone knows that there's no plate like chrome for the Hollandaise!"

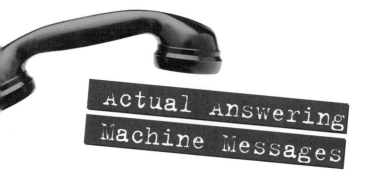

Actual Answering Machine Messages

A is for academics, B is for beer. One of those reasons is why we're not here. So leave a message.

• • •

Hi. This is John. If you are the phone company, I already sent the money. If you are my parents, please send money. If you are my financial aid institution, you didn't lend me enough money. If you are my friends, you owe me money. If you are a female, don't worry, I have plenty of money.

• • •

(Narrator's voice) There Dale sits, reading a magazine. Suddenly the telephone rings! The bathroom explodes into a veritable maelstrom of toilet paper, with Dale in the middle of it, his arms windmilling at incredible speeds! Will he make it in time? Alas no, his valiant effort is in vain. The bell has sounded. You must leave a message.

• • •

Please leave a message. However, you have the right to remain silent. Everything you say will be recorded and will be used by us.

• • •

Hi. I'm probably home, I'm just avoiding someone I don't like. Leave me a message and if I don't call back, it's you.

A young couple was invited to a swanky masked Halloween party. The wife came down with a terrible headache and told her husband to go to the party and have a good time. Being the devoted husband, he protested, but she argued and said she was going to take some aspirin and go to bed. She told him there was no need for him to miss the fun. So he took his costume and away he went.

The wife, after sleeping soundly for one hour, awakened without pain, and as it was still early, she decided to go to the party. Because hubby did not know what her costume was, she thought she would have some kicks watching her husband to see how he acted when she was not around.

She joined the party and soon spotted her husband cavorting around on the dance floor, dancing with every woman he could. His wife sidled up to him. She herself was rather seductive, so her husband left his partner high and dry and devoted his time to his new mystery partner.

She let him go as far as he wished (naturally, since he was her husband). Finally he whispered a little proposition in her ear and she agreed, so off they went to one of the cars and had a little interlude.

Just before unmasking at midnight, she slipped out, went home and put the costume away and got into bed, wondering what kind of explanation he would have for his notorious behavior.

She was sitting up reading when he came in, and she asked him what he had done. He said, "Oh, the same old thing. You know I never have a good time when you're not there." Then she asked, "Did you dance much?" He replied, "I'll tell you, I never even danced one dance. When I got to the party, I met Pete, Bill and some other guys, so we went into the den and played poker all evening. But I'll tell you...the guy that I loaned my costume to sure had one helluva time!"

• • •

A boy and his father visiting from a technologically primitive part of the world were at a mall. They were amazed by almost everything they saw, but especially by two shiny, silver walls that could move apart and back together again.

The boy asked his father, "What is this, Father?" The father responded, "Son, I have never seen anything like this in my life. I don't know what it is!"

While the boy and his father were watching wide-eyed, an elderly woman walked up to the moving walls and pressed a button. The walls opened and the woman walked in between them into a small room. The walls closed and the boy and his father watched small circles of lights with numbers above the walls light up. They continued to watch the circles light up in the reverse direction. The walls opened up again and a very shapely young woman stepped out.

The father said to his son, "Go get your mother."

• • •

VAN GOGH'S RELATIVES

The brother who accidentally bleached all his clothes white...
Hue Gogh

The real obnoxious brother...**Please Gogh**

The brother who ate prunes...**Gotta Gogh**

The uncle who worked at a convenience store...**Stop N. Gogh**

His dizzy aunt...**Verti Gogh**

The cousin who moved to Illinois...**Chica Gogh**

His magician uncle...**Wherediddy Gogh**

The cousin who lived in Mexico...**Amee Gogh**

The nephew that drove a stagecoach...**Wells Far Gogh**

The uncle who was constipated...**Cant Gogh**

The aunt who loved ballroom dancing...**Tan Gogh**

His ornithologist uncle...**Flamin Gogh**

His nephew, the Freudian psychoanalyst...**E. Gogh**

His cousin who loved tropical fruits...**Mang Gogh**

And his aunt who taught the power of positive thinking...
Way To Gogh

His bouncy young nephew...**Poe Gogh**

His disco-loving sister...**Go Gogh**

And his niece, who's been traveling the U.S. in a van...**Winnie Bay Gogh**

• • •

If Yoko Ono married Sonny Bono, she'd be Yoko Ono Bono.

If Dolly Parton married Salvador Dali, she'd be Dolly Dali.

If Bo Derek married Don Ho, she'd be Bo Ho.

If Oprah Winfrey married Depak Chopra, she'd be Oprah Chopra.

If Cat Stevens married Snoop Doggy Dogg, hey! it's the '90s!, he'd be Cat Doggy Dogg.

If Olivia Newton-John married Wayne Newton, then divorced him to
marry Elton John, she'd be Olivia Newton-John Newton John.

If Sondra Locke married Elliott Ness, then divorced him to marry Herman Munster, she'd become Sondra Locke Ness Munster.

If Bea Arthur married Sting, she'd be Bea Sting.

If Liv Ullmann married Judge Lance Ito, then divorced him and married Jerry Mathers, she'd be Liv Ito Beaver.

If Snoop Doggy Dogg married Winnie the Pooh, he'd be Snoop Doggy Dogg Pooh.

If G. Gordon Liddy married Boutros Boutros-Ghali, then divorced him to marry Kenny G., he'd be G. Ghali G.

Nog (Quark's brother on "Star Trek: Deep Space Nine") has no other name, so he uses it twice when getting a marriage license. If he married Howard Hughes, and then Pamela Dare, he'd be Nog Nog Hughes Dare.

If Ivana Trump married, in succession, Orson Bean (actor), King Oscar (of Norway), Louis B. Mayer (of MGM), and Norbert Wiener (mathematician), she would then be Ivana Bean Oscar Mayer Wiener.

IN CASE YOU'RE EVER ON A GAME SHOW

The Eisenhower interstate system requires that one mile in every five must be straight. These straight sections are usable as airstrips in times of war or other emergencies.

The Boston University Bridge (on Commonwealth Avenue, Boston, Massachusetts) is the only place in the world where a boat can sail under a train riding under a car driving under an airplane.

The United States government keeps its supply of silver at the U.S. Military Academy at West Point, NY.

Cats have over 100 vocal sounds, while dogs have only about 10.

Our eyes are always the same size from birth, but our nose and ears never stop growing.

David Prowse was the guy in the Darth Vader suit in Star Wars. He spoke all of Vader's lines, and didn't know that he was going to be dubbed over by James Earl Jones until he saw the screening of the movie.

Most Americans' car horns beep in the key of "F."

Many hamsters only blink one eye at a time.

In every episode of "Seinfeld" there is a Superman somewhere.

February 1865 is the only month in recorded history not to have a full moon.

It takes a lobster approximately seven years to grow to be one pound.

Montpelier, Vermont, is the only U.S. state capital without a McDonald's.

No word in the English language rhymes with month.

There are two credit cards for every person in the United States.

Roger Ebert is the only film critic ever to have won the Pulitzer prize.

An iguana can stay under water for 28 minutes.

Leonardo da Vinci invented the scissors.

In the last 4,000 years, no new animals have been domesticated.

Babies are born without knee caps. They don't appear until the child reaches 2-6 years of age.

The highest point in Pennsylvania is lower than the lowest point in Colorado.

If you have three quarters, four dimes, and four pennies, you have $1.19. That's also the largest amount of money in coins you can have without being able to make change for a dollar.

No NFL team that plays its home games in a domed stadium has ever won a Super Bowl.

In the Great Fire of London in 1666, half of London burned down but only six people were injured.

Lincoln Logs were invented by Frank Lloyd Wright's son.

The only two days of the year in which there are no professional sports games (MLB, NBA, NHL, or NFL) are the day before and the day after the Major League All-Star Game.

Only one person in two billion will live to be 116 or older.

THE BEST OF THE WORST
COUNTRY-WESTERN SONG TITLES
(Yes...these are REAL)

1. Drop-Kick Me Jesus Through The Goalposts Of Life
2. Get Your Biscuits In The Oven And Your Buns In The Bed
3. Get Your Tongue Outta My Mouth 'Cause I'm Kissing You Goodbye
4. How Can I Miss You If You Won't Go Away?
5. I Changed Her Oil, She Changed My Life
6. I Fell In A Pile Of You And Got Love All Over Me
7. I Keep Forgettin' I Forgot About You
8. I Wouldn't Take Her To A Dawg Fight Cause I'm Afraid She'd Win
9. I've Been Flushed From The Bathroom Of Your Heart
10. I've Got The Hungries For Your Love And I'm Waiting In Your Welfare Line
11. If I Can't Be Number One In Your Life Then Number Two On You
12. If You Don't Leave Me Alone I'll Go And Find Someone Else Who Will
13. My John Deere Was Breaking Your Field While Your Dear John Was Breaking My Heart
14. My Wife Ran Off With My Best Friend And I Sure Do Miss Him
15. She Got The Gold Mine And I Got The Shaft
16. She Got The Ring And I Got The Finger
17. Thank God And Greyhound She's Gone
18. They May Put Me In Prison But They Can't Stop My Face From Breakin' Out
19. You're The Reason Our Kids Are So Ugly

HOW TO PHOTOGRAPH A PUPPY

1. Remove film from box and load camera.

2. Remove film box from puppy's mouth and throw in trash.

3. Remove puppy from trash and brush coffee grounds from muzzle.

4. Choose a suitable background for photo.

5. Mount camera on tripod and focus.

6. Find puppy and take dirty sock from mouth.

7. Place puppy in pre-focused spot and return to camera.

8. Forget about spot and crawl after puppy on knees.

9. Focus with one hand and fend off puppy with other hand.

10. Get tissue and clean nose print from lens.

11. Take flash cube from puppy's mouth and throw in trash.

12. Try to get puppy's attention by squeaking toy over your head.

13. Replace your glasses and check camera for damage.

14. Jump up in time to grab puppy by scruff of neck and say, "No, outside! No, outside!"

15. Call spouse to clean up mess.

16. Take a breather.

17. Sit back in Lazy Boy with drink and resolve to teach puppy "sit" and "stay" the first thing in the morning.

THE PARROT

So there's this fella with a parrot. And this parrot swears like a sailor, I mean he's a pistol. He can swear for five minutes straight without repeating himself. Trouble is, the guy who owns him is a quiet, conservative type, and this bird's foul mouth is driving him crazy.

One day, it gets to be too much, so the guy grabs the bird by the throat, shakes him really hard, and yells, "QUIT IT!" But this just makes the bird mad and he swears more than ever.

Then the guy gets mad and says, "OK for you" and locks the bird in a kitchen cabinet.

This really aggravates the bird and he claws and scratches, and when the guy finally lets him out, the bird cuts loose with a stream of invective that would make a veteran sailor blush.

At that point, the guy is so mad that he throws the bird into the freezer.

For the first few seconds there is a terrible din. The bird kicks and claws and thrashes. Then it suddenly gets very quiet.

At first the guy just waits, but then he starts to think that the bird may be hurt. After a couple of minutes of silence, he's so worried that he opens up the freezer door.

The bird calmly climbs onto the man's outstretched arm and says, "Awfully sorry about the trouble I gave you. I'll do my best to improve my vocabulary from now on."

The man is astounded. He can't understand the transformation that has come over the parrot.

Then the parrot says, "By the way, what did the chicken do?"

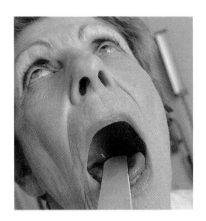

Got more?

Send the dead-tree editions of your jokes to:

Castle Pacific Publishing
2020 Pennsylvania Avenue NW
Suite 187
Washington, DC 20006

Or, e-mail your jokes to:

jokes@castlepacific.com

Include your name and mailing address. Also, tell us if you are the author or if you know who the author might be.

Thanks!